# HASH
# HOUSE

*Lingo*

DOUBLE CONEYS

KER CONEYS                    HAMBURGS

DIER

DINER          *Good*
COFFEE

# HASH HOUSE Lingo

The Slang of Soda Jerks, Short-Order Cooks,
Bartenders, Waitresses, Carhops, and Other
Denizens of Yesterday's Roadside

## Jack Smiley

WITH A NEW INTRODUCTION BY **Paul Dickson**

Dover Publications, Inc. | Mineola, New York

*Copyright*
Copyright © 2012 by Dover Publications, Inc.
Introduction to the Dover Edition copyright © 2012 by Paul Dickson
All rights reserved.

*Bibliographical Note*
*Hash House Lingo: The Slang of Soda Jerks, Short-Order Cooks, Bartenders, Waitresses, Carhops, and Other Denizens of Yesterday's Roadside,* first published in 2012, is an unabridged republication of *Hash House Lingo,* originally published by the author in 1941. The introduction and annotations in the text, both by Paul Dickson, and the vintage illustrations, have been newly added to this Dover edition.

Book design by Scott Russo
Illustrations courtesy of the Scott Russo Archive

*International Standard Book Number*
*ISBN 13: 978-0-486-48112-8*
*ISBN 10: 0-486-48112-3*

Manufactured in the United States by Courier Corporation
48112301
www.doverpublications.com

> ## "But for my own part, it was Greek to me."
> ### —William Shakespeare, *JULIUS CAESAR*

# INTRODUCTION TO THE DOVER EDITION

On an August morning in 1991 I stopped for breakfast at the Deluxe Diner in Rumford, Maine. The first thing I heard was Pete the counterman and owner say.

"Couple a blues with."

"Couple a blues comin' up," said a female voice from the kitchen as Pete drew coffee from the 40-year old coffee machine that he'd fired up at 3:00 that morning (for his 4:00 A.M. customers.) Rose, the waitress, arrived with two monster, homemade "blues with"—blueberry muffins and several pats of butter.

On that summer morning the blues were selling well and a few minutes later Pete asked for one "with wheels"—which meant that it was to be put in a paper bag "to go."

There were a lot of good reasons to stop at this diminutive diner that was, and still is, tucked into a tiny lot on Oxford Street. The food was first rate, the prices were what big city folk paid a decade earlier, and Pete Duguay, the owner, made sure you felt at home even when it was early and the sky was as black as his coffee. In addition to the fact that I was hungry, I was here for the calls—or abbreviated orders—which were hurled about and are as much a part of the culture of diners, luncheonettes, soda fountains and short-order eateries as bread pudding, squeaky stools, and neon-rimmed clocks.

Calls are the distinct form of communication that allows those behind the counter to pass orders around with a degree of efficiency and good humor that is typically American—perhaps as American as Cockney Rhyming Slang is British. The rules are easy: make it whimsical and make it easy to hear so there is no confusion, and no need for repetition.

For this reason, DOWN means "toasted" and BACK means "on the side." A few examples heard at the Deluxe—A.C. for American cheese, as opposed to S.C. for Swiss; ALL THE WAY means a sandwich served with all the fixin's; B AND B is not bed and breakfast but bread and butter, and BOWL OF RED is chili con carne.

These calls were born in 19th century lunchrooms, cafés and saloons, and nurtured in the early 20th century in diners, luncheonettes and soda fountains. Today they are still heard in a handful of the older traditional diners and in a few anomalies like the Waffle House chain in the Deep South, which has its own hash house dialect. But for all intents and purposes, hash house is a dying lingo. If precious little of the original lingo extends to the present time, it still lives on in spirit as an ancestor to 21st century modern slanguages such as the slang of the workers who toil delivering pizza, serving coffee and scooping ice cream at the mall.

Perhaps it went into decline because of the fact that although the terms were colorful they were not always appetizing. As John F. Mariani explains diner and lunch counter slang in his *Dictionary of American Food and Drink,* "... the vitality of lunch-counter speech—CAT'S EYES for tapioca, BABY for glass of milk, JERK for ice cream soda, and ADAM AND EVE ON A RAFT for fried eggs on toast—had a raciness about it that many people sought to put an end to in the late 1930s." As Columbia University linguistics specialist W. Bentley observed in the journal *American Speech* in 1936: "The craze for this sort of fountain entertainment seems to be on the wane. Indeed the practice is frowned upon in many fountains, particularly those owned or operated by large chain organizations or department stores."

*Hash House Lingo* was published in 1941, with the aim to put it all under a single roof from A–Z. Its subject was immediately decried by the industry, which was still trying to stamp it out. A review in the October, 1941 issue of *The Diner,* a trade magazine, saw the book as a "glossary of forgotten (Thank God) terms." The reviewer went on to explain: "This patter was all right in the early days—it was interesting and crude, or perhaps interesting because it was crude. But it led to keen rivalry for the wittiest expressions—countermen would be vying with each other for the most novel way of ordering. Sometimes the stuff was so novel that the chef had to ask for the order 'in English.'" The result, he argued, was that service declined and noise and crudeness increased.

This is Mr. Smiley's original *Hash House Lingo* annotated and very slightly edited by yours truly. Corrections are limited to some obvious typographic errors (B.M.T. in the self-published original instead of B.L.T.) and the removal of a few irrelevancies, which would only detract from the enjoyment of the work.

PAUL DICKSON
*Former part-time soda jerk (1954–1955)*

ACKNOWLEDGMENT: Stanley Fink, and other members of the Easton, Penna., *Morning Free Press* who knew a story when they saw it. Dr. Bentley for parts reprinted here from his *Concoctions of a Soda Jerker*, American Speech, Feb. 1936, by permission of Columbia University Press. S. A. K., who I hope will understand. and most of all, Easy and Richard for bearing with me.

JACK SMILEY
*August 6, 1941*

SPECIAL'S
YELLOW TAILS POTATOES 35
TURTLE STEAK-POTATOE.S 40
CONCH-STEAK-POTATOE.S 35
JEW FISH STEAK-POTATOES 35
KING FISH- POTATOE.S 35
½ FRY OYSTERS-POTATOE.S 45
FILET STEAK-POTATOES 40
HAMBURGER STEAK-POTATOE.S 35
HAM+CABBAGE DINNER 35

# HASH HOUSE LINGO

It is told that Henry Ward Beecher, having been greatly impressed by the originality and the resourcefulness of soda dispensers in coining names of their servings, decided on one occasion to put the slanguistic imagination of one particular dispenser to a test. Upon taking his seat at a lunch counter, Mr. Beecher placed his order for two eggs on toast and then added, "Please scramble them." The challenge was met, so the story goes, without hesitation on the part of the waiter who reeled off to the cook what is now an outworn call, "ADAM AND EVE ON A RAFT AND WRECK 'EM." Whether true or not, this story is no exaggeration of the lengths to which the bright boys behind the marble counters have extended themselves to outdo the other fellow with fantastic, grotesque or witty labels for the food combinations from the kitchen or fountain. While the practice is frowned upon in many places, particularly those owned or operated by large chain organizations, this craze for linguistic entertainment is still very popular. This use of camouflaged language is an attraction in many establishments which have built reputations on it.

There was a time, not long since, and much later than that of Beecher, when the soda jerker's effectiveness was judged in part on the basis of his ability to how off behind the counter with the witty use of such fabricated language. There is still considerable toleration of originality in tagging servings judged by GIVE IT TO HITLER, BLACKOUT FOR TWO, and the like.

If one attempts to explain the origin of the terms and phrases of the soda fountain-restaurant terminology he must frequently resort to conjecture. The dispensers usually admit that they have never concerned themselves with origins or they may offer authoritatively one or more elaborate but naïve explanations. For example, MARY GARDEN is used for citrate of magnesia because it "makes you sing." No doubt a great variety of motives contributed to the situation. There is the possibility that the customer's feelings were considered and that an effort was made to conceal orders rather than broadcast them to other customers. On the other hand, regard for the feelings of customers would seem to have been about the last consideration in the mind of the originator of the unappetizing, even revolting terms applied to some dishes—BLOOD, HEMORRHAGE, DOG AND MAGGOT, BELLY-WASH, for example. It is more than possible that the human trait of showing off to gain attention is responsible for prevalence of much of this smartly substituted terminology. A SLANG SLINGER urged on by an appreciative audience would be induced to bring forth all the fresh expressions his wits might concoct. The fact that he was following the common practice of man to create an argot of picturesque or grotesque, endearing or malicious names for his tools lent a certain sanction to the undertaking.

Another motivation force is the readily understood necessity for a signal system recognizable by insiders of the trade but mysterious to outsiders. When a customer, forgetfully or otherwise starts to leave without paying his bill, it simplifies a difficult situation to call out 95, rather than make a formal complaint. Likewise it eases the nervous tension of employees subject to inspection by an overseer to have the word passed along with an innocent 99 that the manager is around. Numbers are most commonly used for signals, but descriptive terms are also used. While many of these terms do not apply to food, they are used by employees and merit inclusion in this volume, for example, the entrance of a good looking woman is heralded with VANILLA and if she sits in a booth and crosses her legs conspicuously, this is broadcast to employees with 87½.

A great deal of humor is in evidence in many commonplace items such as EVE WITH A LID ON for apple pie, ADAM'S ALE for water, FIRST LADY for spare ribs, DISGUSTED for custard, COW PASTE for butter and COWBOY for a Western sandwich. A lack of dignity is found in DOG BISCUITS for crackers, WARTS for olives, WHISTLE BERRIES, BAND BERRIES, SHOOTERS or MUSICAL FRUIT for baked beans.

It is to be expected that those items most frequently ordered lend themselves more readily than others to the pastime of calling things not what they are but what they resemble or bring to mind. Among those carrying a long list of tags are coffee, water, Coca-Cola and milk. An order for a cup of coffee may be given by any of the following terms: DRAW ONE, AND ANOTHER, BLACK AND WHITE, CUP OF JAVA, CUP OF JAMOCH or DRAW SOME MUD while black coffee is ordered with DRAW ONE BLACK, DRAW ONE IN THE DARK, BLACKOUT FOR ONE, MIDNIGHT, MUG OF MURK or DRAW ONE NO COW.

Expressions signifying Coca-Cola are SHOOT ONE, POP ONE, SHORT COKE, PAUSE or SHOT IN THE ARM, all calling for a small Coca-Cola. Others are HOLD THE HAIL (without ice), MAKE IT VIRTUE (add cherry syrup), SHOOT ONE FROM THE SOUTH (strong), SHOOT ONE AND SPIKE IT (add lemon), VIRGIN COKE (with cherry syrup), WALK ONE or WALK A SHOT for a bottle of Coca-Cola.

Instead of milk the following are used: BABY, BOTTLE, MOO JUICE, COW, 2½ (small glass), 5 (large glass), ONE FROM THE COUNTRY (buttermilk) or the colorful TWIST IT, SHAKE IT AND MAKE IT CACKLE (egg malted milk shake).

A few of the terms used for water are: 81, TIN ROOF, ADAM'S ALE, ONE ON THE HOUSE, CITY GIN, DEW, MOISTURE, CITY COCKTAIL or DOG SOUP.

While this list is of course fragmentary, it contains those terms and phrases most commonly used in fountains, diners and restaurants throughout the country and compiled over a period of years. It will be noted that many of the terms used here have no direct connection to an eating establishment. People from all walks of life frequent these places and terms are concocted by employees to refer to these customers.

**A.C.**—American cheese sandwich

**Ace**—one dollar

**Aches**—eggs

**Acid**—vinegar

**Adam and Eve on a raft**—two poached eggs on toast

This is undoubtedly most common example of Hash House Lingo, especially after the order is placed and the customer requests the order be changed to scrambled and the counterman says "Wreck 'Em." It was so oft quoted that other lines could feed on it. *The Chicago Tribune*, September 30, 1919: "Professor claims he unearthed an egg over 1,000,000 years old. That's how old he estimates it. What year would you say it was laid in? Maybe it was with Adam and Eve on the raft." Synonyms include: A PAIR FLOATING IN THE OCEAN, TWO BIDDIES ON A RAFT and EYES UP.

**Adam's ale**—water

**Aggies**—baked beans

**Agony wagon**—ambulance

**Alleviator**—glass of tomato juice and a cup of black coffee

**Alleluia lass**—Salvation Army worker

**All arms and legs**—weak (said of coffee or soup)

**All black**—chocolate soda with chocolate ice cream

**All hot**—baked potato

**Alligator**—native of Florida

**All to the mustard**—very good

**Alps**—restaurant above the ground floor

**Amen-snorter**—minister

**Ammunition**—toilet paper

**Amscray**—beat it; go away

**Anchor**—wife

**Angel**—sandwich man; financial backer

**Angels on horseback**—oysters rolled in bacon and served on toast

**Ankle**—to walk slowly

**Annie Oakley**—meal ticket

**Apple dumpling shop**—woman's bosom

**Apron up**—pregnant

**Arkansas toothpick**—knife

**Artillery**—baked beans

**Athlete's foot**—stewed dried peaches

**Atlanta Special**—Coca-Cola

**Axle grease**—oleo-margarine

**B and B**—bread and butter

**Baby**—small glass or bottle of milk

**Baby kisser**—politician

**Baby sauce**—mustard

**Backbiter**—deceitful person

**Back scratcher**—one who praises you for your praise of him

**Back teeth afloat**—intoxicated

**Bad breath**—onions

**Bad news**—restaurant check

**Baggage**—wife

**Baked Alaska**—baked Swiss steak

**Baked Bean**—native of Boston

**Bald headed row**—restaurant booths

**Baled hay**—shredded wheat

**Ball and chain**—wife

**Ball of fire**—glass of brandy

**Balloon juice**—seltzer

**Bang berries**—baked beans

**Bang up**—profitable

**Bank**—cash register

**Banner**—restaurant check

**Bark at the moon**—to sing

**Barked pie**—fruit cobbler

**Barks**—frankfurters

**Barley broth**—beer

**Bar mop**—towel

**Barn stormer**—itinerant restaurant worker

**Base runner**—itinerant restaurant worker

**Beadsteader**—sleepy counterman

**Beagle**—native of Virginia

**Bean buster**—heavy eater

**Bedbug**—amorous person

**Beef**—to complain

**Beef a la mode**—beef stew

**Beef stick**—bone

**Beer slinger**—bartender

**Bees**—American cheese

**Beetle**—policeman

**Beetle blood**—ale

**Beggars**—5¢ and 10¢ checks

**Belch water**—carbonated water

**Belly-aching**—complaining

**Belly-bumper**—physician

**Belly busters**—baked beans

**Belly cheat**—apron

**Belly chokers**—doughnuts

**Belly furniture**—food

**Belly robber**—chef

**Belly timber**—food

**Belly walloper**—physician

**Belly warmer**—cup of coffee

**Bellywash**—beer

**Bender**—an employee having food concealed on his person when leaving his work

**Bending an elbow**—drinking beer at a bar

**Bend the crab**—overcharge a disagreeable person

**Bennie**—overcoat

**Bernice**—aspirin tablets

**Berries**—dollars; eggs

**Bessie**—roast beef

**Better half**—wife

**Bib**—napkin

**Bible**—cook-book

**Biddies on a raft (board)**—poached eggs on toast

**Biddy**—young woman

**Biddy board**—French toast

**Big noise**—restaurant owner

**Bilge water**—soup

**Bim**—young woman

**Bimbo**—young woman

**Bindle stiff**—hobo

**Bing**—small restaurant

**Birdie**—one dollar

**Bird seed**—Grape-Nuts cereal

**Biscuit**—the heart

**Biscuit grabber**—glutton

**Biscuit shooter**—baker

**Bison**—Italian

**Biters**—teeth

**Black and white**—chocolate soda with vanilla ice cream (fountain); cup of black coffee with cream on the side

**Black ball**—discharge from job; chocolate ice cream

**Black bottom**—chocolate ice cream with chocolate syrup

**Black box**—safe (money)

"Eat Your Thanksgiving "Turk" Here: And Save Your Wife For A Pet At Home!

**Black cow**—chocolate milk

**Black gang**—boiler room gang

**Blackleg**—strike-breaker

**Blackout**—black coffee

**Black moo**—chocolate milk

**Black stick**—chocolate ice cream cone

**Black water**—root beer

**Bleat**—complain

**Bleed**—to empty; to overcharge

**Blimp**—stout woman

**Blind pig**—place where liquor is sold illegally

**Blind robins**—fried herring

**Blind tiger**—waterfront restaurant

**Blinkers**—eyes

**Blister**—contemptible person

**Blood**—catsup

**Bloodhounds**—frankfurters

**Blood sucker**—loan broker

**Bloomer**—an unsuccessful enterprise

**Blow in**—arrive; enter

**Blow off**—end; closing time

H 5¢

The CHOICEST PRODUCT OF THE BREWERS' ART

FALSTAFF

Sandwiches
AND LUNCH

**Blow one**—glass of beer

**Blow out**—celebrations

**Blow out patches**—pancakes

**Blow your copper**—to have part of wages retained by management in payment for broken dishes

**Blue Bottle**—Bromo-seltzer

**Blue funk**—nervous apprehension

**Blue Moon**—watered tea served to waitresses and hostesses instead of liquor although customer is paying for liquor

**Blue pencil**—discharge from position

**Blue room**—manager's office

**Blurb**—menu

**Blurb rag**—newspaper

**B. L. T.**—bacon, lettuce and tomato sandwich—
This term is still very much with us as is O.J. for orange juice. Less familiar today are G.J. for grapefruit juice, C.B. for corned beef, and R.B. for roast beef—a call which lives on in the chain of Arby's Restaurants which features R.B.

**Bo**—hobo

**Board**—slice of toast

**Boarding house specials**—prunes

**Bob**—dollar

**Bobtail**—new employee

**Boffle**—one dollar

**Bog top**—fruit cobbler

**Boiled hay**—tea

**Boiled leaves**—tea

**Boiler house**—orchestra pit

**Boiler makers**—musicians

**Bolo**—new employee

**Bonarue**—very good

**Bone crusher**—physician

**Bones**—dollars

**Booing**—dancing

**Boomer**—itinerant restaurant worker

**Boomerang**—worthless check

**Boot**—one that carries tales to the manager

**Booth**—braggart

**Bootleg**—coffee

**Booze school**—saloon

**Bosom fly**—amorous person

**Bossy**—beef

**Bossy in a bowl**—beef stew

**Bossy on a board**—roast beef sandwich on toast

**Bossy powder**—powdered milk

**Bottle**—bottle of milk

**Bottle back**—employee who takes time off from work to attend church services

**Bottled lightning**—cheap corn liquor

**Bottom**—ice cream in a drink

**Bouncer**—worthless check; one who maintains order

**Bovine juice**—milk

**Box**—any stringed instrument

**Brace**—two

BRACE is just the beginning of a sequence for numbers which continues: CROWD—Three orders of anything, as in: "Three's a crowd," BRIDGE—Four orders of an item, from the foursome of a bridge game, HANDFUL—Five orders, from the numbers of fingers on the hand.

**Brain buster**—one who prepares the menus

**Brain stick**—cigarette

**Brand a steer**—fry a hamburger

**Bratter**—child's nurse

**Brazilian cocktail**—coffee

**Bread basket**—the stomach

**Break it and shake it**—add egg to a drink

**Breath**—onion

**Bricks**—biscuits; Jewish style hard rolls

**Brick top**—red haired person

**Brodie**—to take a chance

This term refers to Steve Brodie (December 25, 1861–January 31, 1901,) an American from who claimed to have jumped off the Brooklyn Bridge and survived on July 23, 1886. The newspaper reports at the time gave Brodie lots of publicity, and the tavern he opened shortly afterward was a success. His name entered the language for a period of time as "pull a Brodie" meaning to take a chance. Thus the risk implied in ordering the next item.

**Brodie stew**—beef stew

**Bromide**—an old joke

**Bronx orchid**—cabbage

**Bronx vanilla**—garlic

**Broom**—to leave a job

**Broomstick and pebbles**—frankfurters and beans

**Brown bellies**—raisins

**Brown bottle**—iodine bottle

**Brownies**—pennies

**Brown it up**—cook it well

**B. U.**—biological urge (passion)

**Bubble and squeak**—sauerkraut and pork

**Bucket of suds**—glass of beer; cup of coffee

**Buck pie**—huckleberry pie

**Buckshot**—caviar

**Buck the tiger**—to toss coins to see who pays a check

**Buff**—person's skin

**Bug**—bell used by cook to signal that order is ready to be served

**Bug dust**—smoking tobacco

**Bullets**—baked beans

**Bull horn**—tuba

**Bully beef**—boiled beef

**Bum beef**—unjustified reprimand or complaint

**Bumming**—begging

**Bumper**—drink of liquor

**Bum rap**—false accusation

**Bum steer**—false information

**Bundle of rags**—wife

**Bung hole**—kitchen door aperture

**Bunkie**—roommate

**Burbank**—farmer

**Buried**—working in the back room of a restaurant

BURN. Omitted from Jack Smiley's original Hash House Lingo is an entry for burn meaning to cook. This call can be disconcerting if one is not prepared for it. A friend of the annotator who was born in Scotland and moved to the U.S. as a young man loves to tell the story of the first time he ate in an American diner and heard a waitress call across the room and tell her counterman to "Burn the British." He recalls, "I didn't realize she was asking for a toasted English muffin, and for one very quick moment I thought I'd stumbled on some hotbed of anti-British feeling."

**Burn a snow-ball**—dip of chocolate ice cream

**Burner**—drink of cheap liquor

**Burn it and let it swim**—chocolate float

**Burn one all the way**—chocolate malted with chocolate ice cream

**Burn up the bull**—well done steak

**Busting beans**—eating

**Butcher**—vendor

**Butzo**—signal warning of the approach of an unwanted person

**Buzzer**—cigarette lighter

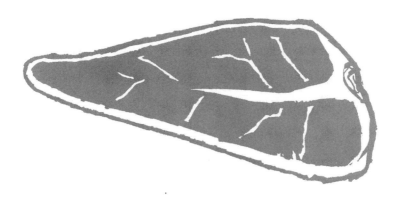

**c**—cheese

**C note**—$100.00 bill

**Cabbage**—$1.00 bill

**Cackle berries**—eggs

**Cackle crate**—poultry box

**Caddies**—bus boys

**Cage**—kitchen

**Cake cutter**—cashier that shortchanges customers

**Call down**—reprimand

**Can**—discharge from a position

**Canary**—porter; singer

**Canary Island**—vanilla soda with chocolate ice cream

**Can it**—shut up

**Canned cow**—evaporated milk

**Cannibal sandwich (steak)**—raw chopped beef sandwich (steak)

**Canoodle**—to make love to one of the opposite sex

**Cape Cod turkey**—salted codfish

**Carfare**—$5.00

**Carp**—letter from management that is read and signed by each employee

**Carpet bagger**—lazy counterman

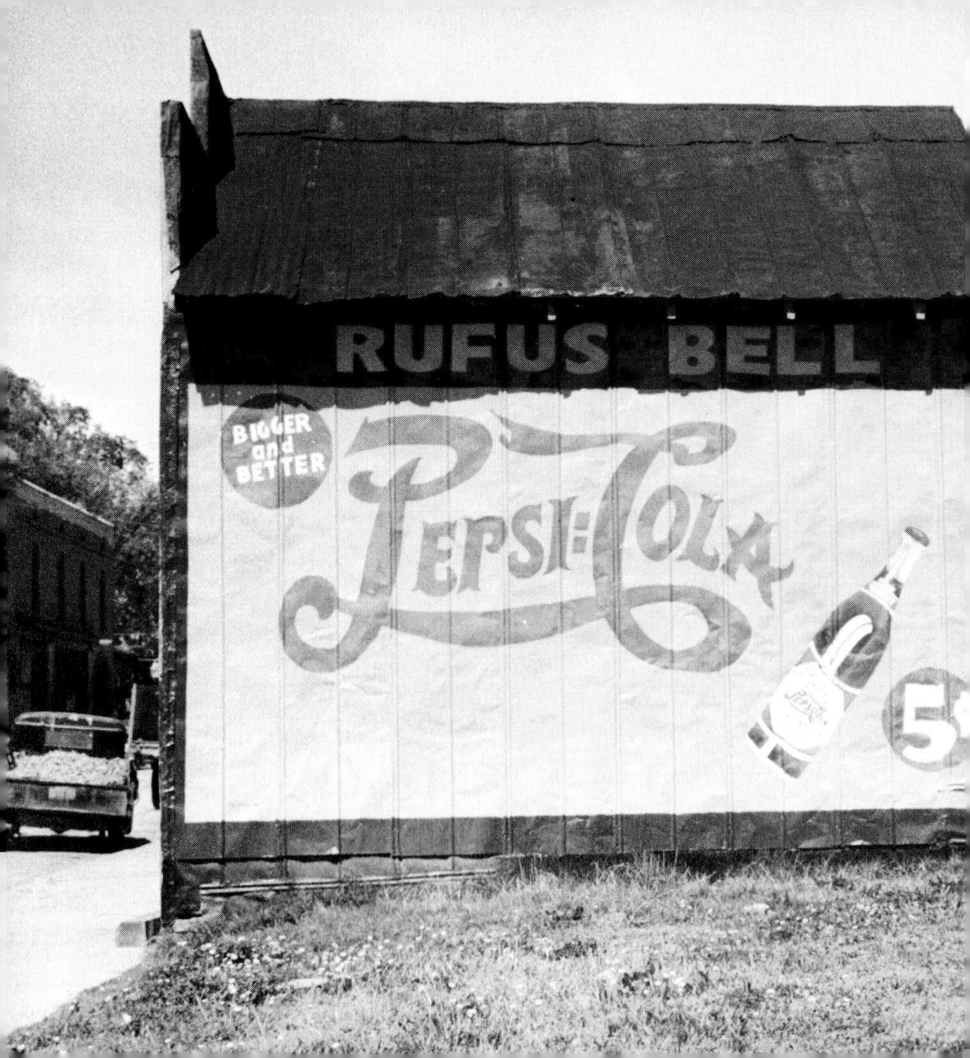
RUFUS BELL
BIGGER and BETTER
Pepsi-Cola
5

**Carrot top**—red headed person

**Carry the banner**—stay awake

**Cartwheel**—silver dollar

**Case**—to watch another employee so as to learn how to do a task

**Catching the monkey**—necking

**Cat's eyes**—tapioca pudding

**Cat soup**—catsup

**Caught in a snowstorm**—under the influence of dope; said of a cook that can't remember orders

C.B. is your cheeseburger while your double cheeseburger is C.B.2. These calls were heard by the annotator at the Deluxe Diner in 1991.

**C.C.**—cream cheese

**Celebrity**—fountain man that is popular with women

**Chase**—pass (verb)

**Chase the pangs**—eat

**Chewed fine with a breath**—hamburger with onion

**Chi**—Chicago

**Chicago**—pineapple sundae

**Chicago shake**—pineapple milk shake

**Chicken berries**—eggs

**Chicken feed**—silver money

**Chief crook**—restaurant bookkeeper

**Chin**—to talk

**China clipper**—dish washer

**Chin fest**—women's banquet

**Chin gang**—tea room customers

**Chin mower**—razor

**Chink**—money.

**Chinky**—to tie knots in a new employee's clothes while they are in his clothes locker

**Chippy**—young woman

**Chits**—counterfeit coins

**Choc hi**—chocolate malted milk

**Choked beef**—hamburger

**Choke holes**—doughnuts

**Choke one**—hamburger

**Choker**—hamburger; large amount of money

**Chokies**—artichokes

**Chopper**—knife

**Chow burner**—cook

**Chuck**—food; to wear clothes

**Chuck horrors**—indigestion

**Ciggy**—cigarette

**Cincinnati chicken**—fried salt pork

**Cincy**—Cincinnati

**Circus**—night club

**City cocktail**—water

**City juice**—water

**C.J. Boston**—cream cheese and jelly sandwich on brown bread

**C.J. white**—cream cheese and jelly sandwich on white bread

**Clampers**—fingers

**Claret**—blood; catsup

**Claw hammer coat**—full dress suit

**Claws**—fingers

**Clean**—without funds

**Clean up the kitchen**—hamburger steak; hash

Other sources suggest that this term was more commonly a specific reference to corned beef hash. In 1928 when Prince William of Sweden took a rail tour of America in a Pullman car, which he writes about in the November issue of *The Living Age* magazine, he comments on the slang of the waiters in the dining car. When he ordered corned beef hash with a poached egg on top he hears "Clear up the kitchen and put a rose on it."

**Clinchers**—fingers

**Clinkers**—biscuits

**Clip joint**—high priced restaurant

**Cloud**—food checker; headwaiter

**Clove foot**—slow worker

**Coast**—to drink a large amount of liquor

**C. O. Cocktail**—castor oil served at fountain

**Codbank**—Boston

**Codfish**—well dressed diners

**Coff**—coffee

**Coffee and**—coffee and doughnuts

**Coffee grinder**—taxi

**Coffee pot**—small all night restaurant; taxi

**Coffin nail**—cigarette

**Combo**—combination sandwich; small orchestra

**Coney Island bloodhounds**—frankfurters

**Coney Island chicken**—frankfurters

**Connie**—tubercular employee

**Conniption fits**—sudden outburst of anger

**Cooked socks**—stewed dried peaches

**Cookie joint**—tea room

**Cookie pusher**—wealthy young woman

**Coosey**—cook; some fountain men apply this term to a loose woman

**Cootie**—counterfeit coin; also used for body lice

**Cop a mope**—to leave a place of employment on a personal errand without the manager's permission

# CHIPETA CAFÉ

**STEAK-TROUT and CHICKEN DINNERS**

*Coffee, the cream of*

**Cop a plea**—acknowledge a complaint

**Copesettee**—all right

**Corn willy**—canned corned beef

**Corset**—fountain man's short work coat

**Couch beetle**—amorous person

**Counter jumper**—counterman

**Country club**—morgue

**Court plaster**—dollar bill

**Cow**—milk; fat woman

**Cowboy**—Western sandwich

**Cowboy on a raft**—Western sandwich on toast

**Cowcumber**—pickle

**Cow feed**—lettuce

**C. O. White**—cream cheese and olive sandwich on white bread

**Cow juice**—milk

**Cow paste**—butter

**Cow powder**—powdered milk

**Crack a bottle**—open a bottle

**Cracker**—native of Georgia

**Cracker box**—taxi

**Cracker special**—whipped Coca-Cola and ice cream

**Crash wagon**—ambulance

**Cream de goo**—milk toast

**Creep**—glass of beer; non-tipper

**Crime stew**—beef stew

**Croaker**—physician

**Crossbones**—physician

**Crumb castle**—restaurant

**Crush party**—necking party

**Cry cherries**—onions

**Crying towel**—cloth napkin

**Cuddle cutie**—prostitute

**Culls**—hash

**Cup grease**—oleo-margarine

**Cup of lace**—hot chocolate

**Cup of mud**—cup of coffee

**Curbie**—waitress giving curb service

**Curry**—comb

**Cuter**—quarter (twenty-five cent piece)

**Cut throat**—landlord

**C.W. White**—cream cheese and walnut sandwich on white bread

**Damper**—cash register
**Darwin's nose**—hindmost extremity of a chicken
**Dash of lavender**—a female impersonator is coming in the door
**Dawn Patrol**—young woman who patronizes a restaurant regularly in the early morning hours
**Dead beat**—non-tipping customer
**Dead head**—non-tipping customer
**Deck**—unit of anything (box, pkg., slice)
**Decked out**—well dressed
**Deemer**—dime
**Deke**—minister
**Demi-tasse**—prostitute
**Demi-rep**—prostitute
**Deuce**—two dollar bill
**Devil chaser**—minister
**Devil cheater**—minister
**Devil dodger**—minister
**Dew**—water
**Diaper**—cloth napkin
**Dinah**—grease pot
**Ding**—beg

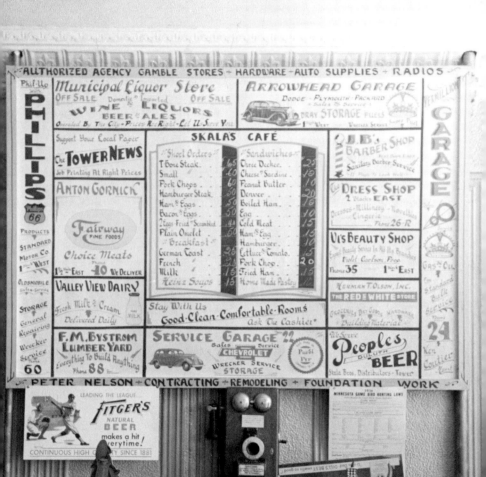

AUTHORIZED AGENCY GAMBLE STORES ~ HARDWARE ~ AUTO SUPPLIES ~ RADIOS

**PHILLIPS 66**
Phillips
PRODUCTS
of
STANDARD
MOTOR Co
1" WEST
OLDSMOBILE
Sales & Service
STORAGE
General
Repairing
Wrecker
Service
60

## Municipal Liquor Store
OFF SALE    Domestic & Imported    OFF SALE
WINE & LIQUORS
BEER & ALES
Operated By The City ~ Prices Right ~ Let Us Serve You

## ARROWHEAD GARAGE
DODGE ~ PLYMOUTH ~ PACKARD
~ Sales & Service ~
DAY STORAGE FUELS
1" West

### Support Your Local Paper
The TOWER NEWS
Job Printing At Right Prices

### ANTON GORNICK
Fairway
FINE FOODS
Choice Meats
1½ EAST  40  We Deliver

### VALLEY VIEW DAIRY
Fresh Milk & Cream
Delivered Daily

### F.M. BYSTROM LUMBER YARD
Everything To Build Anything
Phone 88

## SKALAS CAFÉ

| ~ Short Orders ~ | | ~ Sandwiches ~ | |
|---|---|---|---|
| T Bone Steak | .65 | Three Decker | .25 |
| Small | .40 | Cheese & Sardine | .10 |
| Pork Chops | .60 | Peanut Butter | .10 |
| Hamburger Steak | .50 | Denver | .20 |
| Ham & Eggs | .50 | Boiled Ham | .10 |
| Bacon & Eggs | .50 | Egg | .10 |
| 2 Eggs Fried Scrambled | .45 | Cold Meat | .15 |
| Plain Omelet | .60 | Ham & Egg | .15 |
| ~ Breakfast ~ | | Hamburger | .10 |
| German Toast | .26 | Lettuce & Tomato | .15 |
| French | | Pork Chop | .20 |
| Milk | .15 | Fried Ham | .15 |
| Heinz Soups | .15 | Home Made Pastry | |

Stay With Us
Good ~ Clean ~ Comfortable ~ Rooms
Ask The Cashier

## SERVICE GARAGE
Sales    Service
CHEVROLET
WRECKER SERVICE
STORAGE
Pabst
Pyt

### J.B.'s BARBER SHOP
Sanitary Barber Service

### The DRESS SHOP
2 Blocks EAST
Dresses ~ Millinery ~ Novelties
Lingerie    Phone 26-R

### VI's BEAUTY SHOP
Phone 35    1" EAST

### HERMAN T. OLSON, INC.
The RED & WHITE Store
Groceries ~ Dry Goods ~ Hardware
Building Material

We Serve
**Peoples**
DULUTH
**BEER**
State Bros. Distributors ~ Tower

**GARAGE**
Gas & Oil
Standard
Battery
Service
24
Ken
Coutier
Local

PETER NELSON ~ CONTRACTING ~ REMODELING ~ FOUNDATION WORK

**Dining room lumber**—toothpicks

**Dip**—soup

**Diploma**—raise in wages

**Dirt chaser**—janitor

**Dishwater**—soup

**Dive**—place of ill-repute

**Do a Brodie**—to fall

**Do a casey**—faint

**Do a figure eight**—faint

**Dodge**—a good idea

**Dog and maggots**—crackers and cheese

**Dog biscuits**—crackers

**Dog catcher**—police officer who eats in a restaurant without paying for it

**Dog soup**—water

**Dog wagon**—diner

**Dolly**—large glass of beer

**Donagher**—toilet

**Doodlebug**—subway train

**Dope stick**—cigarette

**Dopple**—awkward person

**Do a Houdini**—hide when the boss is approaching

**Double O**—here comes the boss; look

**Doughnut**—wealthy person

**Dough well done with cow to cover**—buttered toast

**Down neck**—city slums

**Down the hatch**—garbage can; of no further use or value

**Down yonder**—below the Mason-Dixon line

**Drag**—dance attended exclusively by female impersonators

**Drag a snowball**—chocolate ice cream

**Drag one through Georgia**—Coca-Cola with chocolate syrup

**Draw one**—cup of coffee

**Draw one black**—cup of black coffee

**Draw one in the dark**—cup of black coffee

This from *Life*, the humor magazine; September 26, 1912: A certain waitress who managed to attend a social function succeeded in hiding her identity from all of the party with the exception of one young man. She was telling a coterie of young men and women about her aristocratic family connections and adding that her father and mother were from the best families. "Ham and—draw one in the dark," yelled the mischievously inclined one. The young woman lost her cue. "Coming" she yelled, assuming the position of a waitress."

**Dress a cackle**—make an egg sandwich

**Dress a pig**—make a ham sandwich

Another commonly used word for ham in short-order talk was GRUNT. The late William Safire once wrote about the disappearance of this lingo in his "On Language" column in the *New York*

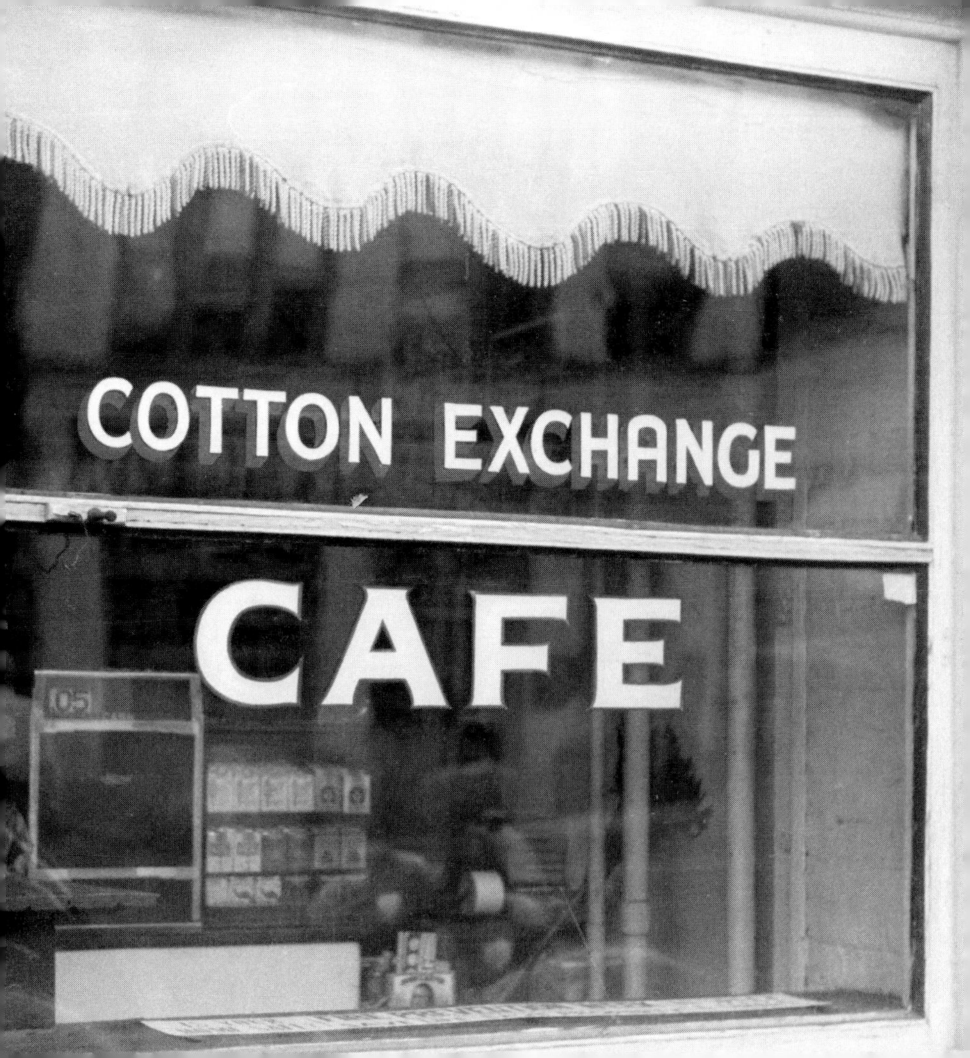
COTTON EXCHANGE
CAFE

*Times* where he wrote that he got on line in fast food restaurant and thought of saying: A CLUCK AND A GRUNT ON A BURNED BRITISH. But he bit his tongue and dutifully murmured: "Egg McMuffin." (*Times.* October 19, 1980.)

**Dress a squeal**—make a pork sandwich

**Dress a yardbird**—make a chicken sandwich

**Dress Bossy**—make a beef sandwich

**Drunken John**—person that can easily be overcharged

**Dry**—sober

**Dry mystery**—hash

**Ducat**—meal ticket

**Duck party**—wedding

**Duffer**—bread

**Duke**—to short change a customer by holding a coin in the palm of the hand while counting out change

**Duker**—meal ticket

**Dukie**—lunch put up to take out

**Dusty Miller**—chocolate sundae; whisky and soda

**Duzey**—a very good thing

**Dynamiter**—fountain man that is a good salesman

DRINK

Coca-Cola

DRINK

Pepper

SPARK PLUG

5¢

**Eagle**—paymaster

**Eagle dirt**—wages

**Eagle is waiting**—customer is waiting to pay his check

**Eagle nest**—cash register

**Echo**—repeat order

**Elbow**—detective

**Engineer's confetti**—toilet paper

**Eskimo highball**—ice water

**Ether**—telephone

**Eve with a lid on**—cut of apple pie

A reference to the biblical Eve's tempting of Adam
with an apple, the "lid" is the pie crust.

**Eye opener**—castor oil in sarsaparilla

**Fall guy**—one who is unjustly accused

**Fancy man**—fountain man

**Fanning the breeze**—gossiping

**Fanny cooler**—restaurant stool

**Fanny parker**—restaurant stool

**Fatback**—salt pork

**Feed**—meal

**Feedbag**—meal; restaurant

**Feeder**—waiter

**Feed the pigs**—eat sparingly

**Feelers**—fingers

**Fem**—young woman

**Fever**—girl friend

**Filling**—meal

**Filly**—young woman

**Fin**—five dollars

**Finagler**—one who hesitates until someone else pays the bill

**Finch**—employee that steals gum and other small items from a restaurant

**Finger**—one who carries tales to the boss

**Fink**—one who carries tales to the boss

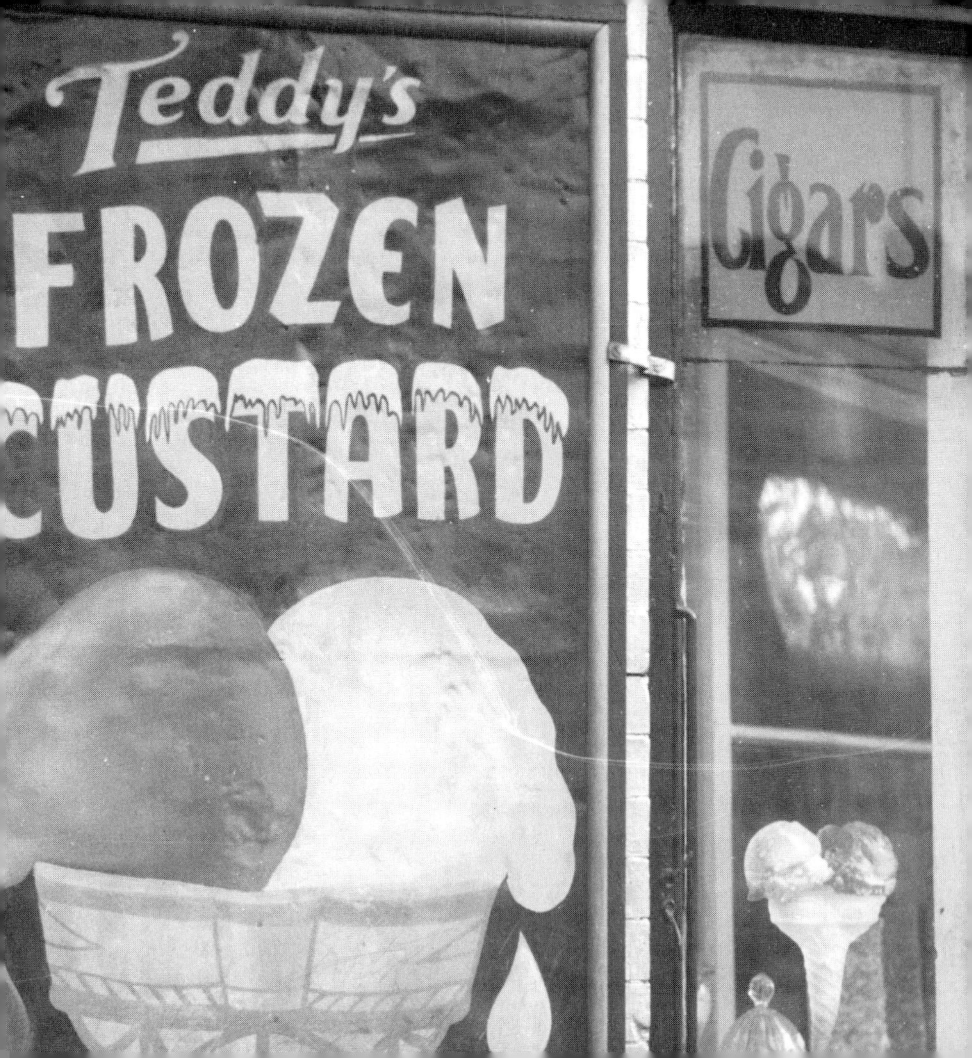
Teddy's
FROZEN
CUSTARD
Cigars

**Finker**—left-over food served to tramps

**First lady**—spare ribs

An allusion to the extra rib that Adam gave to create woman in Genesis. A 1912 compilation of restaurant slang contained this call: SHORTY BROWN IN SWIMMING for short ribs with brown gravy.

**First story worker**—salesman

**Fish eggs**—tapioca pudding

**Fish eyes**—tapioca pudding

FIVE B's—all used in parts of New England for Boston baked beans and brown bread (it is an example of a regional call.)

**Fix**—to look or stare

**Fixer**—attorney

**Fix the frail**—look at the good looking woman

**Fix the gams**—look at the nice legs on that woman

**Fix the knockers**—look at the nice breasts on that woman

**Fix the pumps**—look at the nice breasts on that woman

**Fizzle**—poor paying diner job

**Flannel foot**—manager

**Flannel mouth**—one who carries tales to the boss

**Flapdoodle**—streetcar

**Flaps**—order of wheat cakes

**Flasher**—diamond

**Flash in the pan**—fast fountain man

**Flea bag**—mattress

**Flippers**—the arms

**Floater**—itinerant restaurant worker

**Flop two**—two fried eggs, turned over

**Floozie**—prostitute

**Flop**—to lay down to sleep; place to sleep

**Flowing Mississippi**—coffee

**Flunkey**—janitor

**Fly cake**—raisin cake

**Fly pie**—raisin pie

**Fly punk**—raisin bread

**Fly up the creek**—to leave a place of employment owing borrowed sums to employees

**Fodder**—food

**Follow the cows**—to quit a job and leave town

**Foreign entanglements**—Italian spaghetti

**Forever and ever**—hash

**Forever and the day after**—hash

**Forty miler**—itinerant restaurant worker

**Four bits**—fifty cents

FRESH OYSTERS DAILY

SPAGHETTI & MEAT BALL

OYSTERS ANY STYL

Sandwiches All kind

HOT HAMBURGER

**Frail**—young woman
**Frame**—accuse falsely
**Frankie**—twenty-five cent piece
**Freeze**—ice cream
**Freeze one**—chocolate frosted
**Freeze unto**—take hold of
**Fresh fish**—new employee
**Freshie**—newsboy
**Fresh meat**—new employee
**Frill**—young woman
**Frisco special**—steamed shrimp
**Frisk**—to search the clothing
**Frogged up Murphies**—french fried potatoes
**Frog pie**—french apple pie
**Frog sticker**—carving knife
**Frog sticks**—french fried potatoes
**Front**—persons attire
**Frost**—cracked ice
**Frost one**—frosted Coca-Cola
**Frying pan**—cornet
**Frump**—critical female customer

**Fry one (2)**—fry one (2) eggs with yolks unbroken

**Fry two, let 'em shine**—fry two eggs with yolks unbroken

**Fry two, let the sun shine**—fry two eggs with yolks unbroken

**Fudge**—cheat; overcharge a customer

**Funeral pie**—raisin pie

**Furnace**—kitchen

**Furs**—money taken by a hostess from an intoxicated customer

**Fuzz**—policeman

**Gab-joint**—tea room patronized exclusively by women

**Gab-fest**—women's club meeting

**Gaffer**—manager

**Gallery**—restaurant booths

**Galley**—kitchen

**Galley bum**—cook

**Galley louse**—dish washer

**Gallinipper**—bedbug

**Galloping goose**—street car

**Gallows**—suspenders

**Gam**—leg

**Gander**—look or stare; eye(s)

**Gandy dancer**—itinerant restaurant worker

**Gash**—young woman

**Gas house**—saloon

**Gazers**—spotters

**Gee-gee**—race horse

**Gelt**—money

**Gentlemen will take a chance**—hamburger steak; hash

**George Eddy**—non-tipping customer

**Georgia chicken**—salt pork

**Georgia pie**—peach pie
**Georgia special**—Coca-Cola
**Get off**—to stop whatever one is doing
**Get outside of**—to eat or drink
**Get the mittens**—to be discharged from a job for stealing
**Ghost patrol**—spotters
**Gid**—young woman
**Giddyap**—person's walk
**Giggle fizz**—champagne
**Giggle soup**—champagne
**Giggle water**—champagne
**Gilly**—prostitute
**Gimp**—dishonest employee
**Gin-gay**—gingerbread

Golden
WAFFLES

*Just Covered With*
BUTTER & MAPLE SYRUP

**Give it to Adolph**—throw it into the garbage can

**Give it to Hitler**—throw it into the garbage can

*Hash House Lingo* was published weeks before America was drawn into the Second World War and contains anti-Hitler calls. If there was a direct and immediate carryover of this language in the wake of the book's publication it was that a new and powerful slang which appeared within months of the date in 1941 when *Hash House Lingo* was published. It came in the form of the slang of the English-speaking Armed Forces of the Second World War which had irreverent and non-official names for every commonplace in their lives lead by that which came out of the mess halls, chow lines and ration packages. The terms are not always the same but the spirit of them is. Milk is not only known as BABY, BOTTLE, MOO JUICE, and COW but now also as CAT BEER, while condensed milk is now ARMORED COW or TINNED COW. The machines used to create milk from powdered milk and water in areas where fresh milk is not available is now known as MECHANICAL COW.

**Give it to the hogs**—throw it into the garbage can

**Glad rags**—dress clothes

**Glad stick**—cigar

**Glim**—light bulb; eye

**Glimmers**—eyes

**Glob**—dish of vanilla ice cream

**Glom**—steal

**Glory hole**—kitchen

**Glue**—tapioca pudding

**Goat milk**—bock beer

**Gob stick**—clarinet

**Go down Moses**—very cheap liquor

**Gods**—customers using booths

**Go for a walk**—put up an order to take out

**Gold brick**—lazy worker

**Gold dust**—sugar

**Gold fish**—canned salmon

**Gon**—steal

**Goobs**—peanuts

**Gooing**—necking

**Goose**—to tickle

**Goose party**—wedding dinner

**Gopher**—farmer

**Gorp**—eat greedily

—Modern meaning of this is for a mixture of nuts, seeds, dried fruits, bits of chocolate, etc. eaten by hikers for quick energy. Some claim GORP is an acronym for Good Old Raisins and Peanuts but many would side with the late William Safire, who concluded that the acronym story is bunk. Safire has written, "To me, the word seems formed like Lewis Carroll's creation of *chortle* by combining *chuckle* with *snort*; *gorp* is a wedded *snort* and *gulp*." Also its appearance in a 1941 glossary would suggest that it is not an acronym.

**Goy**—gentile

**Grab joint**—quick lunch stand

**Grade A**—bottle of milk

**Grand**—$1000.00

**Grand on a plate**—dish of baked beans

**Grass**—lettuce

Grass was also a call for sauerkraut. When in 1939 there was an attempt to keep these calls from being used in better restaurants one of the offending orders cited was a call for DOGS IN THE GRASS for frankfurters and sauerkraut. (*Los Angeles Times*. October 1, 1939.)

**Gravel**—sugar

**Gravel train**—sugar bowl

**Graveyard stew**—milk toast

For the uninitiated: Buttered toast, sprinkled with sugar and cinnamon, and dropped into a bowl of warm milk. When Hash House Lingo was published it was considered to have curative powers, much as chicken soup is today.

**Grays**—crullers

**Grease**—butter

**Grease ball**—short-order cook

**Greased rope**—an unsuccessful restaurant

**Grease joint**—cheap restaurant

**Grease spot**—hamburger

**Grease the rails**—slander

**Green house**—police station

**Grog**—beer

**Grouch bag**—purse

**Ground**—to discharge from a position

**Ground hog**—frankfurter
**Grouse**—prostitute
**Growler**—large glass of beer
**Grub**—food
**Guess water**—soup
**Gush**—extravagant
**Gypsy foot**—hobo

**Hackney**—clam chowder

**Hack shover**—taxi driver

**Hail**—cracked ice

**Hair pie**—rhubarb pie

**Hair stew**—stewed rhubarb

**Half a yard**—$50.00

**Half seas over**—intoxicated

**Handle**—person's name

**Hand me downs**—ready-made clothes

**Handout**—lunch put up in a bag for a tramp

**Harlem shake**—chocolate milk shake

**Harlem special**—fried chicken

**Harness bull**—uniformed police officer

**Harp**—Irishman

**Hash**—food

**Hasher**—waiter or waitress

**Hash factory**—restaurant

**Hash pie**—mince pie

**Hash slinger**—waiter

**Hay**—shredded wheat cereal

**H. C.**—ham and cheese sandwich

**Head buster**—patrolman's nightstick

**Heat is on**—boss is in a bad humor

**Heaven dust**—cocaine

**Hebrew enemies**—pork chops

**Heebs**—pork chops

**He has a little garden on his stomach**—dead

**Hell cats**—musicians

**Hell cheater**—minister

**Hello girl**—telephone operator

**Hemorrhage**—catsup

**Hen fruit**—egg

**Hep**—aware of

**Hiberny**—corned beef

**High diver**—dishwasher

**High jumper**—young woman fond of liquor

**Highway steak**—frankfurter

**High yellow**—chocolate soda with vanilla ice cream

**Hip gee**—one who thinks he knows it all

**Hipster**—a know-it-all

**Hit bottom**—add ice cream

**Hoboken special**—pineapple soda with chocolate ice cream

**Hog**—garbage can

**Hold the hail**—do not put any ice into it

**Holy Joe**—religious person

**Honey wagon**—garbage wagon

**Honky-tonk**—cheap night club

**Hoof**—dance or walk

**Hootinanny**—automatic phonograph

**Hope**—oatmeal

**Hopper**—bell hop

**Hops**—malted milk; beer

**Hot cha**—hot chocolate

**Hot one**—bowl of chili

Like so many of these calls there are other synonyms: BOWL OF FIRE was noted in a 1948 Baltimore Sun article on counterman lingo, and BOWL OF RED was so common in Texas that this was the title that the late Frank X. Tolbert gave to his definitive work on the subject. Cecil Smith wrote in the *LA Times* in recalling the diner calls of his childhood: "Chili and beans had a place in the language too. I particularly remember the dish being called the MEXICAN NAVY and BOWL OF FIRE. One restaurant dubbed it DEATH IN THE AFTERNOON. (*Los Angeles Times*, April 28, 1953.)

# LITTLE SU

## BEER ON TAP

Cafe

We Serve
Nation
BEER

PABST

NATIONAL
BEER and
ALE

PABST

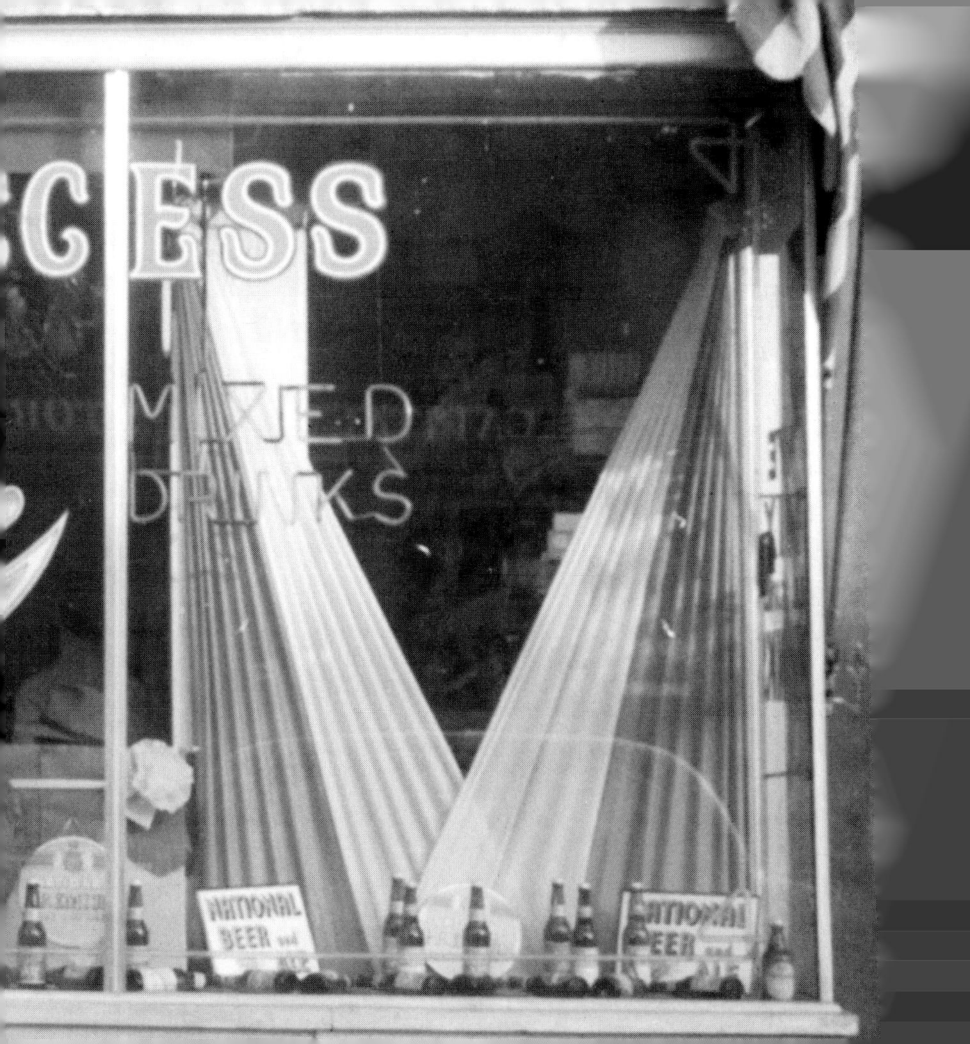
CESS
NATIONAL
BEER and
NATIONAL
EER

**Hot sauce**—mustard

**Hotscotch**—out of the way diner

**Hot top**—hot chocolate

**Hounds on an island**—frankfurters and beans

Another common call for this is FBI. What does the I stand for? Nothing. FBI sounds better than FB.

**House boat**—banana split

**Hudson River ale**—water

**Hugger**—glass of orange juice

**Hug one**—glass of orange juice

**Hula pie**—pineapple pie

**Humming bird**—talkative fountain man

**Hump**—Camel cigarette

**Hungry House**—restaurant

**Hunk of lead**—doughnut

**Hurricane**—garlic

**Huskie**—one who maintains order in a club

**Hypo**—overcharge

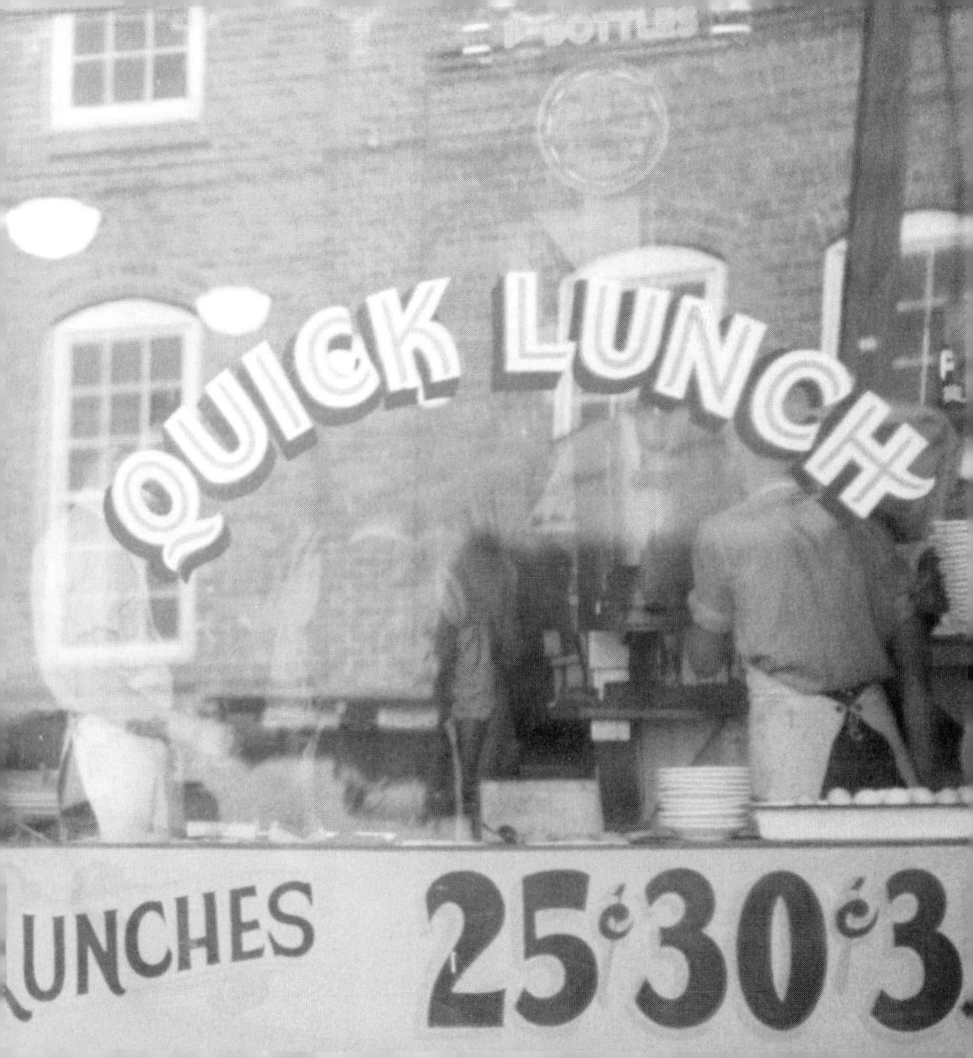
QUICK LUNCH
LUNCHES
25¢ 30¢ 3

**Iceberg**—refrigerator

**Ice cart**—ambulance (morgue)

**Iceman**—coroner

**Ice on rice**—rice pudding with ice cream

**In a clinch**—married

**In a jackpot**—in trouble

**Inhale**—to eat or drink

**In soak**—owing money; in pawn

**In the hay**—strawberry flavor

**Irish cherries**—carrots

**Irish cutlet**—baked haddock

**Irish goldbricks**—sweet potatoes

**Irish terriers**—white potatoes

**Irish turkey**—corned beef

**Iron hat**—derby hat

**Iron pants**—chaste woman

**Italian hurricane**—spaghetti with garlic sauce

**Italian storm**—spaghetti with garlic sauce

**Jack**—bus boy

JACK. Can also stand for grilled American cheese which works out to G.A.C. but the call is JACK.

**Jack knife**—to fall

**Jack leg**—personnel manager

**Jailbait**—teen age girls

**Jakey**—Jamaica ginger liquor

**Jamboree**—fight among customers

**Jamoka**—coffee

**Jarbox**—taxi

**Jarvey**—taxi driver

**Java**—coffee

**Jawbone**—credit

**Jay**—farmer that collects garbage

**Jay jump**—church

**Jeepy**—foolish

**Jennie**—waitress

**Jingle-bob**—union button worn by employees

**Jit**—five cent piece

**Jizzie**—unattractive woman

**Jockey**—cashier

**Joe**—coffee

**Joe Below**—5 cent restaurant

**Joe McGee**—person that runs out without paying check

**Joey**—comical fountain man

**Johnnies**—Philip Morris cigarettes

**Jones boys**—salt and pepper shakers

**Juke box**—automatic phonograph

**Jumpy**—police radio car

**Jump over the broomstick**—marry

**Jungle rum**—cheap liquor

**Juvie**—child

**Kale**—money

**Kelsey**—young woman

**Kicking the gong around**—sitting (employees) around and talking because of the lack of customers

**Kip**—sleep

**Kip Liz**—prostitute

**Kipper**—all right

**Kiwi**—prostitute

**Kiyoodle**—police officer

**Know the beans**—be aware of

**Kudo**—good standing with the management

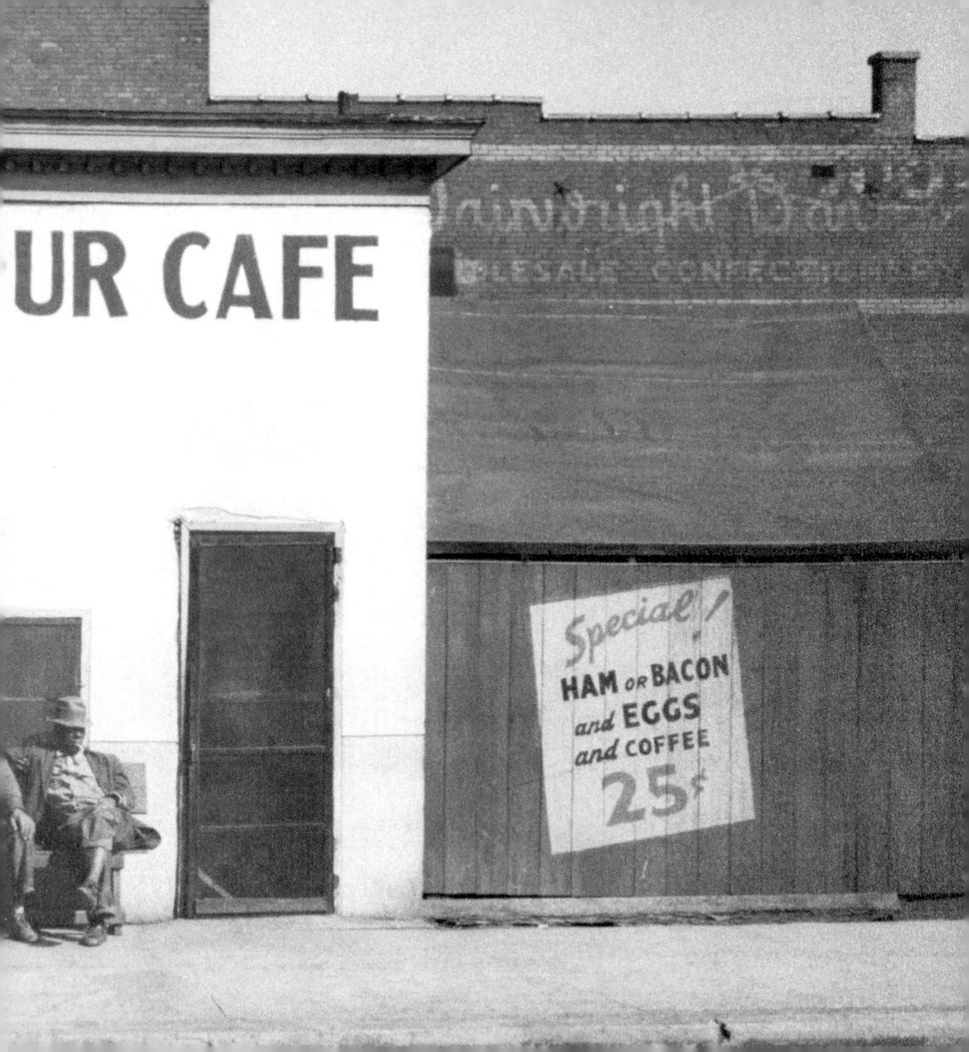
UR CAFE
Special!
HAM OR BACON
and EGGS
and COFFEE
25¢

**Lacey up**—hot chocolate
**Lady bug**—fountain man popular with the women customers
**Lam**—run; to quit a job
**Lame stick**—crutch
**Lame talk**—alibi
**Lamps**—the eyes
**Lark**—prostitute
**Laugh soup**—champagne
**Lead pipe**—spaghetti
**Leather**—purse
**Leather breeches**—dried kidney beans
**Leaves**—lettuce
**Leg off a pair of drawers**—draw two cups of coffee
**Leg off one**—cup of coffee
**Lemon squeezer**—night club hostess
**Let it walk**—put up an order to take out
**Let the sun shine**—fry 2 eggs with yolks unbroken
**Life boat**—increase in salary
**Life preservers**—doughnuts
**Lighthouse**—bottle of catsup
**Light stick**—match

**Limejuicer**—Englishman

**Lingo**—slang; language

**Lion**—fountain man popular with customers

**Lip**—lawyer; spokesman for employees

**Lizard**—steady customer

**Load of**—order of anything

**Lob**—dishwasher

**Long**—signifies large order

**Looking at daisy roots**—dead and buried

**Loony bins**—rest room for women

**Looseners**—prunes

**Loose water**—epsom salts solution

**Lord**—head fountain man

**Lounge lice**—customers that spend a long time at a fountain over a 5¢ drink

**Louse house**—rooming house

**Louse lady**—rooming house landlady

**Lousyliz**—cheap prostitute

**Love apple**—tomato

**Love box**—booth

**L.T.**—lettuce and tomato sandwich

SANDWICHES

Ka-vee ICE CREAM

*Pallas*

RESTAURANT

**Lubie**—sweetheart

**Lumber**—toothpick

**Lush**—intoxicated

**Lynx**—women employee that carries tales to the boss

**Madwag**—talkative fountain man

**Maggot**—cheese

**Mahaskas**—waitress that gives in easily to male employees while at work

**Maiden juice**—cherry syrup

**Maiden pie**—cherry pie

**Maiden's delight**—cherries

**Main drag**—principal street of a city

**Main gee**—manager

**Main line**—restaurant

**Main squeeze**—hostess

**Main stem**—principal street of a city

**Make a break**—to stop what one is doing

**Make it virtue**—add cherry syrup

**Makings**—tobacco and paper used in rolling one's own cigarettes

**Mama**—marmalade

**Mama on a raft**—marmalade on toast

**Manhattan cocktail**—dose of castor oil in sarsaparilla

**Map**—person's face

**Marble orchard**—cemetery

**Mary Garden**—dose of magnesia with water chaser (makes you sing)

**Match**—toss coins to see who pays a check

**Mats**—pancakes

**May**—mayonnaise

**McGee**—not fresh

**Meal ticket**—job; husband

**Mealy mouth**—fault finding customer

**Meatball**—Italian

**Meatwagon**—ambulance

**Meow session**—women's club meeting

**Merry widow**—street car

**M. G. Cocktail**—dose of magnesia

**Mick**—Englishman

**Mickies**—sweet potatoes

**Midget from Harlem**—small chocolate soda

**Midnight**—cup of black coffee

**Mike and Ike**—salt and pepper shakers

**Mile a meal**—plate of spaghetti

**Milkman's matinee**—breakfast dance (which is usually lewd)

**Milksop**—effeminate fountain man

**Million on a platter**—plate of baked beans

**Minnow**—young woman

STAR CAFE
DRINKS - STAR CAFE
Cafe
OLD GOLD
Chesterfields are milder
SAFETY FIRST
PHILIP MORRIS
124-677

**Minx**—prostitute

**Miscue**—make an error

**Mississippi mud**—mustard

**Miss Nancy**—effeminate fountain man

**Mistake**—fried liver

**M. M. Cocktail**—dose of magnesia

**Mocking bird**—singing waiter

**Moisture**—water

**Mollies**—trade coins

**Mongrel**—police officer

**Monkey**—dish washer

**Monkey dish**—ice cream plate

**Monkey parade**—the social set

**Monkey suit**—full dress suit; waiter's uniform

**Mooch**—beg

**Moo juice**—milk

**Moola**—milk

**Moonshine**—rice

**Mope**—stupid person

**Moss back**—conservative eater

**Mother McCrea**—hard luck story

**Mousing**—necking

**Mountain apples**—onions
**Mountain dew**—cheap liquor
**Mountain oysters**—sweetbreads
**Mouse**—bruised eye
**Mouthpiece**—lawyer
**Moxie**—courage
**Mrs. Grundy**—landlady
**Mud**—chocolate pudding; black coffee
**Muddy eyed**—near-sighted
**Mud punk**—whole wheat bread
**Muffin fight**—tea party
**Mugbug**—girl that gives in easily
**Muggles**—champagne
**Mug of murk**—cup of black coffee
**Mully**—beef stew
**Murphy**—potato
**Mush cootie**—cockroach
**Musical fruit**—baked beans
**Musiker**—musician
**Mystery**—hamburger roast
**Mystery stew**—beef stew

**Nance**—effeminate man
**Napoleon**—$20.00 bill
**Narrow back**—dishwasher; cashier
**Navvy**—dish washer
**Nervous pudding**—gelatin pudding
**N. G.**—no good
**Nickel nurser**—miser
**Nickel chaser**—subway (New York)
**Night rider**—police car doing night patrol duty
**Nine spokes**—silly person
**Nipper**—bus boy
**Nippy**—waitress
**Noah's boy**—boiled ham
**Noah's boy with Murphy carrying a wreath**—Boiled ham
and cabbage with potatoes
**Noble**—waitress
**Nose**—spotter
**Nubbins**—spoiled food
**Nurse**—to use sparingly

**Oakley**—free meal

**O'Connors**—potatoes

**Off the reel**—added to an order to signify a "rush order"

**Oh gee**—orange juice

**Oil**—tip; praise

**Old Army standby**—baked beans

**Oldie**—adult

**Old maids**—prunes

**On a bat**—on a drinking spree

**On a bender**—on a drinking spree

**One arm joint**—small cheap restaurant

**One from Boston**—order of baked beans

**One from the Alps**—Swiss cheese sandwich

**One from the cannibals**—chopped raw beef sandwich

**One from the country**—glass of buttermilk

**One from the South**—Coca-Cola

**One from Texas**—order of tamales

**One in all the way**—chocolate soda with chocolate ice cream;
hamburger with all the trimmings

**One in the dark**—cup of black coffee

**One on**—hamburger

**One on the house**—glass of water

**One up**—this signifies an order of one, usually the most popular item sold as beer, hamburgers, hot dogs, etc., while "one down" refers to an order of one, of the second most popular item, thus "one up" "one down" could mean a glass of beer and a glass of ale or it could mean a hamburger and a hot dog. Each restaurant or fountain usually has its own meaning for these two terms.

**Onion**—inexperienced fountain man

**On the arm**—on credit

**On the ball**—"hurry that order"

**On the blink**—spoiled

**On the bum**—begging

**On the carpet**—being reprimanded

**On the cuff**—on credit

**On the double**—"hurry that order"

**On the Erie**—a warning, signifying that someone is listening

**On the fire**—busy; "your order is being prepared"

**On the in**—in a position to learn first hand information

**On the kibosh**—of no further value

**On the make**—usually applied to a woman who is seeking male companionship

**On the mooch**—begging

**On the muscle**—angry

**On the pan**—being reprimanded

**On the prowl**—eavesdropping

**On the Q. T.** —in a quiet manner

Conspicuous by its absence from the original Hash House Lingo was the term ON WHEELS for a take-out order and of course TO GO. There were more elaborate constructions: DRESS ONE PIG TO GO FOR A WALK for a take-out ham sandwich.

**On the stem**—begging

**O. O. or Double O**—"look"; to stare at

**Ork**—orchestra

**Pail**—cup
**Painters**—red kidney beans
**Paint one**—cherry Coca-Cola
**Pair of drawers**—two cups of coffee
**Pajama wagon**—sleeper bus
**Palm**—to steal small articles (gum, candy) by concealing them in the palm of the hand
**Pan**—the face; criticize adversely
**Pan cake**—silver dollar
**Pan joint**—cafeteria
**Parson's nose**—hindmost part of a chicken
**Party slum**—mixture of spaghetti and beans (Italian pasta-va-zoo)
**Patsy**—all right
**Pause**—Coca-Cola
**Pay your rent**—stop bothering with the women and get to work
**Paznazki**—loose woman
**Pea buster**—fast eater
**Pearl diver**—dish washer
**Pebbles**—baked beans
**Pegged down**—married
**Perch**—diner stool

**Perk**—coffee

**Pest**—assistant manager

**Pete box**—safe

**Phiz**—person's face

**Pick me up**—loose woman

**Pie pusher**—inexperienced counterman

**Piffle**—rhubarb

**Pigeon milk**—cream (scarcity)

**Pig in a wreath**—ham and cabbage

**Pig and a pillow**—ham sandwich on a roll

**Pig between sheets**—ham sandwich on sliced bread

**Pig in a blanket**—frankfurter sandwich

**Pig is fat**—everything is all right

**Pig joint**—barbecue stand

**Pig salve**—lard

**Pig sticker**—carving knife

**Pill chaser**—nurse

**Pill party**—stay in a hospital

**Pill peddler**—druggist

**Pill shooter**—physician

**Pilot house**—church

**Pimp stick**—cigarette

**Pin a rose on it**—add onion to it

**Pink one**—free meal

**Pink stick**—strawberry ice cream cone

**Pipe**—stare; look

**Pirate**—landlord

**Pitch till you win**—eat all you can

**Pittsburgh**—food is burning; cup of black coffee

**Plaster**—$1.00

**Play the piano**—take money from register

**Plow jockey**—farmer

**Poison pan**—assistant manager

**Poke**—purse

**Poker**—toothpick

**Polar bear**—ice man

**Pony**—small drink of liquor

**Pooch**—police officer

**Pop boy**—inexperienced fountain man

**Popeye**—spinach

**Pop one**—fountain Coca-Cola

**Poppagoy**—talkative person

**Porkville**—Chicago

**Pot belly**—chef

**Pot smasher**—dish washer

**Pot wrestler**—dish washer

**Pounding the breeze**—talking

**Pounding the ear**—sleeping

**Program**—menu

**Prune palace**—boarding house

**P.T.**—pot of tea

**Puff**—undue praise

**Pullet**—young woman

**Punk**—bread

**Pushing the clouds around**—dead

**Push water**—gasoline

**Put a chink on ice**—glass of iced tea

**Put a hat on it**—add ice cream.

**Put a hicky in the keyhole**—to close a restaurant for non-payment of rent

**Put on a stepin**—signifies the order is to be taken out

**Put out the lights and cry**—order of liver and onions

**Put out the lights with a squeal (pig)**—order of liver and bacon

**Put the bing on**—beg

**Put the hyp on**—overcharge

**Put the lid on**—to close a restaurant because of poor business

**Put on the feedbag**—eating

**Putting on the nosebag**—eating

**Put to bed with a shovel**—dead

**Put yourself outside of**—to eat or drink

**Q.T.**—stop talking, the boss is coming

**Quail**—Hungarian goulash

**Queen**—hostess

**Queer**—to err or cause to err; degenerate

# NOTICE

## MEAL HOURS
BREAKFAST 7:30 to 8:30 A.M.
SUPPER 4:30 to 5:30 P.M.
SUNDAYS & HOLIDAYS
at 12:00 to 12:45 NOON
❖ COME EARLY ❖

LODGING for 25 MEN
BED TICKETS GIVEN OUT at 6 P.M.

GOSPEL MEETINGS Every Night 7:30 P.M.

RETIRE 8:30 P.M.

OFFICE: SECOND DOOR on IOWA ST.
ask for WILL MASTERS.

**Rabbit food**—lettuce

**Race horse**—cockroach

**Radio**—telephone

**Radio sandwich (salad)**—Tuna fish sandwich (salad)

A play on tuner or the admonition to "tuner down." Dan Carlinsky noted in a 1971 *New York Times* article on the slang of Greek diners that this term was still very much in play (*New York Times*, September 5, 1971.)

**Raffle berries**—eggs

**Raft**—slice of toast

**Rag**—newspaper

**Rags**—paper currency

**Rallybank**—church

**Rasp**—razor

**Rat dance**—unjustified reprimand

**Rat gut**—cheap liquor

**Rat poison**—cheap liquor

**Rattler**—railroad train

**Rattle the cup**—carry tales to the boss

**Reader**—license to operate a business

**Ream**—young woman

**Red ball**—apple; orangeade

**Red cap**—porter

**Red devils**—kidney beans

**Red eye**—cheap unaged liquor

**Red horse**—corned beef

**Red hot**—frankfurter

**Red lead**—catsup

**Red legs**—cockroaches

**Redlight**—to discharge from a position

**Red merk**—corned beef

**Red merk and violets**—corned beef and cabbage

**Red noise**—tomato soup

**Red onion**—well educated fountain man

**Red paint**—catsup

**Red top**—catsup

**Repeaters**—baked beans

**Rhinelander**—chocolate soda with vanilla cream

**Rib**—female

**Rib smasher**—physician

**Ridge-runner**—bell hop

**Riot act**—reprimand

**Roach cake**—raisin cake

**Roaches**—raisins

**Roll**—to pick the pockets of an intoxicated person

**Root**—cigar

**Root beer special**—dose of castor oil in root beer

**Rose**—onion

**Rough diamond**—irresponsible and wealthy young person

**Rubber neck**—tourist

**Runner**—food order to be delivered

**Rush it**—Russian dressing

**Sack**—to discharge from a job
**Salt horse**—corned beef
**Salve**—butter
**Sand**—sugar
**Saturday nights**—baked beans
**Saturday night special**—hostess easily dated by customers
**Saw**—knife
**Sawbones**—physician
**Sawbuck**—$10.00 bill
**Sawdust**—cornmeal; tobacco
**Sawdust and blankets**—tobacco and papers used in rolling one's own cigarettes
**Scandal soup**—vegetable soup
**Scarecrow**—doorman
**Scatter**—small night club
**Schmaltz**—praise
**School House**—State liquor store (by way of Alcoholic Beverage Control)
**Schooner**—large glass of beer
**Scoff**—eat
**Scoff joint**—restaurant

**Scoop**—spoon

**Score card**—menu; restaurant check

**Scratch**—coins

**Scratcher**—match

**Screech box**—violin

**Scuttle butt**—drinking fountain

**Scuttler**—shoplifter

**Sea berries**—beans

**Sea dust**—salt

**Sea gull**—chicken

**Sea sand**—salt

**Self starter**—glass of tomato juice and cup of black coffee

**Set**—order of bread and butter

**Set down**—good meal

**Set up**—table eating utensils

**Shaft**—leg

**Shag**—dance attended exclusively by female impersonators

**Shake**—to search

**Shake one**—milk shake (plain)

**Shake one and drag it through Harlem**—chocolate milk shake

**Shake one in the hay**—strawberry milk shake

**Shake the dice**—to betray

**Shamus**—not genuine

**Shanty**—bruised eye

**Sharpshooter**—one who tries to court someone else's friend of the opposite sex

**Shavetail**—new employee

**Shekel**—dollar

**Shell**—small beer

**Shepherd**—head waiter

**Shimmy**—jelly

**Shingle**—toast

**Shiv**—knife

**Shivering Eve**—apple jelly

**Shivering hay**—strawberry gelatin

**Shivering Liz**—mixed flavor gelatin

If you added whipped cream to the order this became SHIVERING LIZ IN THE SNOW.

**Shivering Mick**—lime (green) gelatin

**Shivering virgins**—cherry gelatin

**Shoemaker**—inexperienced employee

**Shoot**—to pass

**Shoot a Grade A**—pass a bottle of milk

**Shoot a pair and spike 'em**—two Coca-Colas with lemon syrup

**Shooters**—beans

**Shooting snipes**—picking up cigarette butts

**Shoot it yellow**—Coca-Cola with much lemon syrup

**Shoot one**—fountain Coca-Cola

**Shoot one from the South**—double strength Coca-Cola

**Shoot one in the red**—Coca-Cola with cherry syrup

**Shoot your mouth off**—to speak out of turn

**Shot**—drink of liquor

**Shot in the arm**—Coca-Cola

**Shot out of the Blue Bottle**—dose of Bromo-seltzer

**Shovel**—spoon

**Shuteye**—sleep

**Shylock**—pawn broker

**Siberia**—refrigerator

**Side arms**—salt and pepper shakers

**Sidecar**—wife

**Sidekick**—partner

**Sin buster**—minister

**Sing small**—lower one's popularity

**Sin eaters**—those attending a Communion breakfast

**Sinkers**—doughnuts

One of the oldest terms in *Hash House Lingo*, it begins to appear with regularity in accounts of waiter slang in the late 19th century.

**Sinkers and suds**—coffee and doughnuts

**Sin pie**—apple pie

**Sin sauce**—apple sauce

**Sitting in booth No. 13**—dead

**Sitting on your ear**—idle

**Six bits**—seventy-five cents

**Sixes and sevens**—free-for-all fight

**Skelly**—master key

**Skid grease**—butter

**Skins**—dollars

**Skipper**—manager

**Skookum**—good; all right

**Sky juice**—water

**Sky lights**—person's eyes

**Sky pilot**—minister

**Slab of**—piece of

**Slab of baaah**—veal sandwich

**Slab of moo**—beef steak

**Slab of moo chewed fine**—hamburger steak

**Slab of moo, let him chew it**—rare beef steak

**Slam off**—die

**Slang slinger**—fountain or counterman using slang terms when ordering food

**Sleeper**—night shift employee

**Sleeping partner**—partner that takes no active part in an enterprise

**Sleigh ride special**—vanilla cornstarch pudding

**Slice of squeal**—slice of ham

**Slicer**—knife

**Sling ink**—to create publicity

**Slough**—close prematurely by law or financial failure

**Slugfest**—boxing match

**Slum**—poorly prepared food; to eat in a cheap restaurant; cheap jewelry

During the American Civil War this was a term for a stew, also known as *slumgulliom* which was created from whatever was at hand. The term appears to be a pure Americanism that first showed up during the gold rush of 1849, when, according to H. L. Mencken in *The American Language, Supplement 1* (1945), it was used to describe a muddy residue left after sluicing gravel; but it was soon extended to food and drink.

**Slum burner**—cook

**Slum diver**—one who patronizes cheap restaurants

**Slum joint**—cheap restaurant

**Slush**—hash

**Smart money**—well dressed person

**Smear**—oleo

Also, butter and, of course, cream cheese from the Yiddish-derived *schema;* a small amount of any condiment applied to a food item.

**Smid**—frugal meal

**Smidget**—counterfeit coin

**Smoke**—black coffee

**Smoke brain**—waiter or counterman that cannot remember orders

**Smoke weed**—tobacco

**Smoking Bishop**—bottle of cheap liquor

**Smooching**—employee making love to one of the opposite sex while on duty

**Smut ghosts**—vice squad

**Smut hounds**—vice squad

**Snag**—young woman

**Snappers**—beans

**Sneeze**—pepper

**Snicker knee**—cleaver

**Snow**—ice

**Snowball**—dip of vanilla ice cream

**Snow shoe**—hot chocolate

**Soak shop**—pawnbroker's office

**Sod buster**—farmer

**Soldier**—loiterer; to shirk duty

**Song and dance**—alibi

**Sop**—gravy

**Soup and fish**—full dress suit

**Soup jockey**—waitress

**Souvenir**—stale egg

**Sparkle one**—dose of Bromo-seltzer

**Sparrow**—asparagus

**Spear**—fork

**Speed ball**—employer's urge to work faster

**Spider grass**—asparagus

**Spike**—(bar) add liquor to a drink; (fountain) add lemon syrup to a drink

**Spiker**—lemon phosphate

**Spill**—railroad station

**Spinner**—silver dollar

**Spirit**—financial backer

**Spla**—whipped cream

**Splash**—soup.

**Splasher**—soup ladle

**Splash of red noise**—bowl of tomato soup

**Splash of splits**—bowl of split pea soup

**Splash of wind**—bowl of bean soup

**Splash out of the garden**—bowl of vegetable soup

**Split**—loose woman

**Split one**—banana split

**Spoil two**—scramble two eggs

**Spondulix**—money

**Spook**—spotter

**Spow**—coffee

**Sprinkle it**—add spirits of ammonia

**Spudder**—vegetable man

**Spuds**—potatoes

**Square**—good meal

**Squawk car**—police radio car

**Squeal sandwich**—ham sandwich

**Squeeze**—orange juice

**Squirrel juice**—thin soup

**Squirt**—fountain man

**Squff**—eat heavily

**Stack**—order of wheat cakes

**Starch**—courage

**Step off**—get married

**Stewed socks**—stewed apricots or peaches

**Stick**—match

**Sticker**—knife

**Stiff**—newspaper; non-tipping customer

**Stink**—perfume

**Stink weed**—pipe tobacco

**Stoker**—fast eater

**Stony**—without funds

**Stormy**—smelling strongly of garlic

**Strap**—pocket

**Straw in**—add strawberry ice cream

**Stretch it**—make it a large order

**Striker**—match

**Struggle for life**—knife

**Submarine turkey**—fish

**Suds**—beer

**Suds buster**—dish washer

**Sugar**—money

**Sugar report**—letter to or from a girl friend

**Suicide jockey**—driver of explosives truck

**Sun kiss**—orange juice

**Susies**—black eyed peas

**Swallow the anchor**—marry

**Sweepings**—hash

**Sweep the kitchen**—plate of hash; hamburger steak

**Sweet 16**—cherry pie

**Sweet Alice**—milk

**Swelling the breeze**—gossiping

**Swill**—beer

**Swindle sheet**—expense account

**Syringe**—meringue pie

**Tabloid**—toilet paper

**Take a chance**—hash; hamburger

In context:

FIRST CUSTOMER—I'll have a plate of hash.

WAITRESS—Gentleman wants to take a chance!

SECOND CUSTOMER—I'll take the same.

WAITRESS—Another sport! (*The Chicago Tribune*, November 21, 1951)

**Take a powder**—abandon

**Take a runout powder**—abandon

**Tanglefoot**—intoxicating liquor

**Tar**—black coffee

**Tar berries**—baked beans

**Tark**—young woman

**Team of grays**—2 crullers

**Tear jerker**—hard luck story

**The long green**—paper money

**The works**—the extreme of anything

**Thick**—friendly

**Thistle chin**—hobo

**Throw in the towel**—quitting a job

**Throw it in the mud**—add chocolate syrup

**Tickle box**—piano

DRINK
**JAX**

EHI
BEVERAGES

ICE C

# GUS'
# CAFE

Hot Cakes *and*
Coffee 10
Stew 10
Chile 10
Hamburgers 5
6 for 25

**Tied**—married
**Tin box**—safe
**Tin roof**—water
**Tintype**—cheap car
**Tipper**—Rabbi
**Tires**—doughnuts
**Toast two on a slice of squeal**—order of ham and eggs
**Toby**—comical fountain man
**Tonsil artist**—singer
**Tools**—table eating utensils
**Torch**—match
**Touch**—loan
**Tout**—lazy employee
**Tray joint**—cafeteria
**Tray tosser**—bus boy
**Trilby**—ham and cabbage
**Trouble**—restaurant check
**Turnip**—watch
**Twelve alive on a shell**—12 raw oysters on the half shell
**Twins**—salt and pepper shakers
**Twist**—young woman

**Twister**—key

**Twist it, choke it and make it cackle**—egg chocolate malted milk shake

**Two U boats and a bale of hay**—franks and kraut

**Uncle**—pawnbroker

**Uncle Bennie**—pawnbroker

**Up**—is usually added to another as "coffee up" "waitress up" or "bread up" and designates the want or approach of a person or thing

Commonly applied to an egg, fried on one side (Sunnyside up) as in two up." On the other hand-DOWN means toasted—an order of DOWN SMEARED would translate to buttered toast.

**Up front**—manager's office

**Upstairs guy**—office worker

**Van**—vanilla ice cream

**Vanilla**—(signal) a nice looking girl is coming in the front door

**Vermont**—maple syrup

**Vichy water**—seltzer

**Violets**—cabbage

**Virgin ball**—dip of cherry ice cream

**Virgin coke**—Coca-Cola with cherry syrup

**Virgin dust**—paprika

**Virgin juice**—cherry syrup

**Virgin pie**—cherry pie

**Virgins**—cherries

**Virtue Island**—tea room

**Virtue pie**—cherry pie

**Wagon**—diner

**Walk a...**—order to take out

**Walk a shot**—bottle of Coca-Cola

**Walk one**—bottle of Coca-Cola

**Wart**—olive

**Washday soup**—bean soup

**Wave the bloody shirt**—antagonize

**Wax**—American cheese

**Waxy**—well-educated

**Weed**—tobacco

**Weed stick**—cigarette

**Weenies**—frankfurters

**Western**—Coca-Cola with chocolate syrup

**Wet mystery**—beef stew

**Whistle berries**—beans

**Whistlers**—beans

**White bread**—danger signal designating the approach of the boss

**White cow**—milk

**White moo**—milk

**White stick**—cone of vanilla ice cream

**Whiz Bang**—waitress easily dated by customers

**Whopper jawed**—talkative

**Wimpy**—hamburger

**Windies**—beans

**Windows**—eye glasses

**Wing ding**—woman's hat

**Wiper**—handkerchief

**Wish book**—mail order catalog

**Witch water**—salt solution used as a cathartic

**Wolf**—lady's man

**Wooden shoe**—trolley car

**Working his bolt**—talking

**Working his nut**—thinking

**Working in a tunnel**—working on the night shift

**Worms**—spaghetti

**Wrap yourself around**—eating or drinking

**Wrecked hen fruit**—scrambled eggs

PORK CHOP & EGGS
BACON & EGGS ~ ~ ~
HAMBURGER STEAK & EGGS
SAUSAGE & EGGS
SHORT RIBS & MACARONI 2
BEEF STEW & RICE ~ ~ 2
EGGS & GRITS ~ ~ ~
HOT CAKES ~ ~ ~ 15
HASH & RICE ~ ~ ~

**Yankee feast**—boiled dinner
**Yanker**—dentist
**Yard**—$100.00
**Yard bird**—chicken
**Yellow ball**—orange
**Yellow paint**—mustard
**Yesterday, today and forever**—hash
**Yoik**—farmer
**Yum-Yum**—sugar

**Zombie**—stupid person
**2½**—small glass of milk
**5**—large glass of milk
**13**—boss is close by
**14**—special order
**16 coke**—Coca-Cola with cherry syrup
**21\***—limeade
**22**—check is not paid
**23**—scram; go away
**30**—end of anything
**31\***—lemonade
**36**—cup of Postum
**41\***—small glass of milk
**48½**—discharge from a position
**51\***—hot chocolate
**55½**—small root beer
**66**—empty soup bowl
**73**—best wishes
**81\***—glass of water

81 was also used to indicate that table had not been served and given water and a menu. In an article in *American Speech* on the Jayhawk Café in Lawrence, Kansas, it was noted that regular patrons learned this bit of code and would yell out "81" when they wanted service.

## 86—sold out

86 is still very much with us and not only in terms of restaurant slang but in terms of general 21st century slang in which it means to reject or veto something. Armchair lexicographers have found it puzzling as a stand-alone item—rather than embedded in this 70 year old list with a lot of other numbers which were almost certainly assigned arbitrarily. Explanations abound on the World Wide Web including these:—1. that it was created to rhyme with "nix"; 2. that it derives from British merchant shipping, in which the standard crew was 85, so that the 86th man was left behind; 3. that 86 was the number of a law of some sort that forbade bartenders to serve a person who was drunk; and 4. that a posh New York eatery had 85 tables, so the eighty-sixth was the one you gave to somebody whom you didn't want to serve. There are more, but the point is made that none of this opining would have been necessary if more people knew about Jack Smiley's work.

## 87½—the girl at the table with her legs conspicuously crossed
## 88—love and kisses
## 95—customer leaving without paying
## 98—assistant manager
## 99—Bowl of soup; manager is near
## 400W—maple syrup

* These numbers call for a single unit, so that 22, 32, etc., call for two. 23, 33, etc., call for three and so on.

Come and get it